3

Shadows

When we block light we can make a shadow. Because light travels in straight lines, shadows take the shape of the **opaque** object blocking the light rays.

If you move your hand nearer to the light source the shadow gets bigger. If you move it further away the shadow gets smaller.

Light

Written by Emily Dodd

Contents

Collins

What is light?

Light is a type of **energy**. It can heat things up, make electricity and help plants to grow. It is essential to life.

Light travels in straight lines called rays.

Light rays contain little bursts of energy.

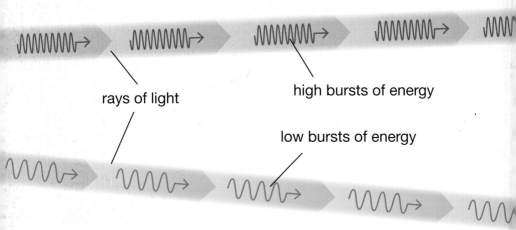

rays of light

high bursts of energy

low bursts of energy

There are many different types of light rays. Humans see light rays as colours. Animals can see light rays that we can't see like **ultraviolet** and infrared.

Our main source of light is the Sun but humans create other sources including lamps, fires and torches. Some animals can make their own light through a chemical reaction in their bodies.

Light travels faster than anything in the Universe.

Tree Shadows

Trees make long shadows in the morning and evening.

Stick a pencil into some modelling clay to represent a tree. Shine a torch on it to represent the Sun's light.

Shine the torch down from above the tree and look at the shadow. It should be very small.

In the middle of the day the Sun is at the highest point in the sky and shadows are at their smallest.

Move the torch to one side and shine it on the pencil. What size is the shadow now? Do the same from the other side.

Towards the end of the day or first thing in the morning shadows are at their longest. This is because of the position of the Sun in the sky.

The Sun appears to move across the sky but really it isn't moving. It is Earth that is turning, and this changes the position of the Sun in the sky.

Fact File

Sun clocks

People used shadows to tell the time long before they had clocks or phones. Ancient Egyptians created big stone clocks called sundials.

The shadow cast on a sundial points at different markings throughout the day. It works like the hour hand on a modern clock.

an ancient Egyptian sundial

Stonehenge is a circle of large standing stones, visited by over a million people every year. Stonehenge was built over 4000 years ago and is a masterpiece of engineering and a wonder of the world.

But what is Stonehenge? Most people today think it was a temple built to make spectacular shadows. **Archaeologists** have noticed the Sun lines up perfectly through the stones stones at sunrise on the summer solstice (the middle day of summer) and sunset in the winter solstice (middle day of winter) so perhaps the circle of stones is a sort of ancient calendar.

Stonehenge, in Wiltshire, England

Reflection

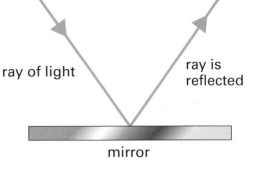

ray of light

ray is reflected

mirror

When light hits an object and bounces back it's called reflection.

Smooth shiny surfaces like mirrors reflect the most light. When you see an object in a flat mirror, light rays are bouncing off the object, then bouncing off the mirror and into your eyes.

Using mirrors

Drivers use mirrors to see what's going on in the road behind them, and to see how far away other vehicles are.

Periscopes use a combination of mirrors cleverly placed which allow us to look round corners or over the top of objects. Submarines use periscopes to see what's above the surface of the water while they stay hidden underwater.

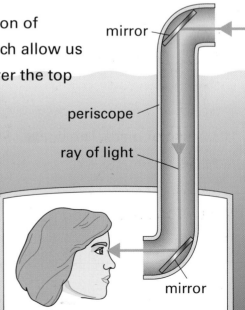

mirror

periscope

ray of light

mirror

Cat's eyes

On a dark and foggy night in 1933, Percy Shaw saw a cat's eyes reflecting in the light from his car headlights. This gave him an idea. He recreated the effect by mounting two pairs of reflective balls into a squishy rubber block. His invention of "cat's eyes" made driving in the dark much safer by lighting up the edges and middle of roads.

Cats have a reflective coating at the back of their eyes which causes light to bounce into their eyes twice. That's why cats can see so well in the dark.

Fact File

Fibre optics

Information can be sent down cables using light. Fibre optic cables are made of plastic or glass. The light reflects off the sides of the cable, bouncing all the way to the other end.

Refraction

Light doesn't just bounce off objects. It can pass through **transparent** and **translucent** objects too.

When light travels from air into another transparent substance like water, it bends and changes direction. The light rays slow down at the point where they meet the new substance and this is what makes the light bend.

This bending of light is known as refraction.

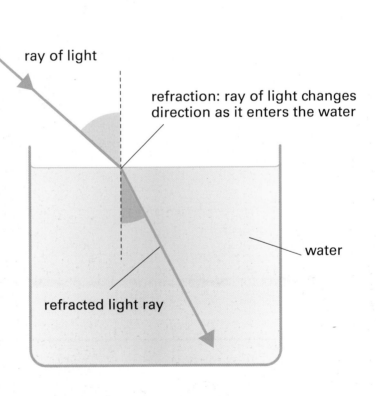

ray of light

refraction: ray of light changes direction as it enters the water

water

refracted light ray

Experiment Refraction

Put a pencil in a tall glass of water. Look at it from above and from the side. What happens to the pencil as it enters the water? How does it change?

The pencil stays straight but because the light bouncing off it is being refracted or bent a little as it travels into the water, it looks as if the pencil is in a slightly different position when the light bounces back into our eyes.

We can bend or refract light in different directions by passing it through different shaped pieces of glass.

Lenses

Lenses are pieces of glass designed to bend or refract light in a useful way.

Convex lenses

Convex lenses are curved outwards on one or both sides so they're thicker in the middle.

They make light rays bend inwards and that makes objects look bigger. Magnifying glasses contain convex lenses.

Microscopes use a series of convex lenses to **magnify** an object many times.

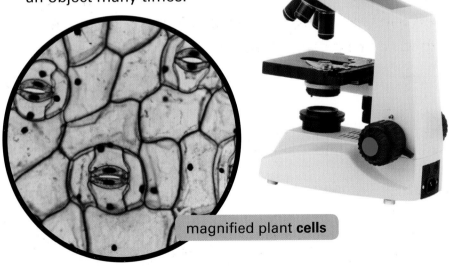

magnified plant **cells**

Cameras use convex lenses to focus the light. A focus is any point where the light rays come together.

convex lens

the rays meet and focus at a point

rays of light

Glasses and contact lenses use convex lenses to help focus the light properly at the back of the eye so that we can see an image in focus.

Concave lenses

Concave lenses are curved outwards on one or both sides so they're thinner in the middle. They make light spread out. They are sometimes used in glasses to make things look smaller so that distant objects look less blurry.

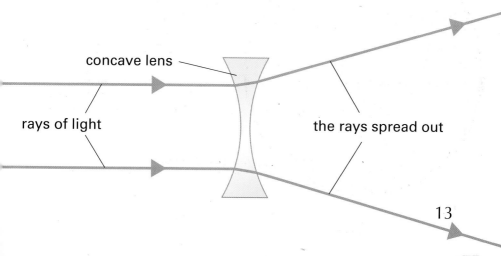

concave lens

rays of light

the rays spread out

13

Seeing light

We can see because light bounces off objects and into our eyes to create images which our brains can understand. But some light is absorbed by objects too.

A leaf looks green because green light is reflecting back at us. Other colours like red and blue are absorbed by the leaf.

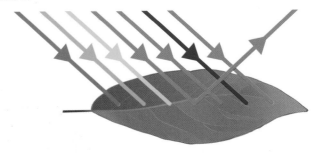

If an object absorbs all light colours it looks black to us. If an object reflects all light colours it looks white to us.

Fact File

In hot countries people wear white clothes because white reflects back most sunlight helping them to keep cool.

What happens when light rays enter our eyes?

Here's how our eyes work:

The coloured part of our eye is called the iris. The iris has a hole in the middle called a pupil and that's where the light travels into the eye.

Behind the iris is a convex lens which helps us to focus the light to make an image of what we're seeing at the back of the eye on the **retina**.

retina

nerve to the brain

rod cell

cone cell

The iris changes the size of the pupil, to let more or less light into the eye. So if it's dark the iris will make the pupil bigger to let in more light. If it's bright, the pupil will become smaller.

Rod and **cone** cells in the retina help us sense the amount and type of light coming from different objects. They send electrical signals to the brain which makes sense of the image.

Rainbows

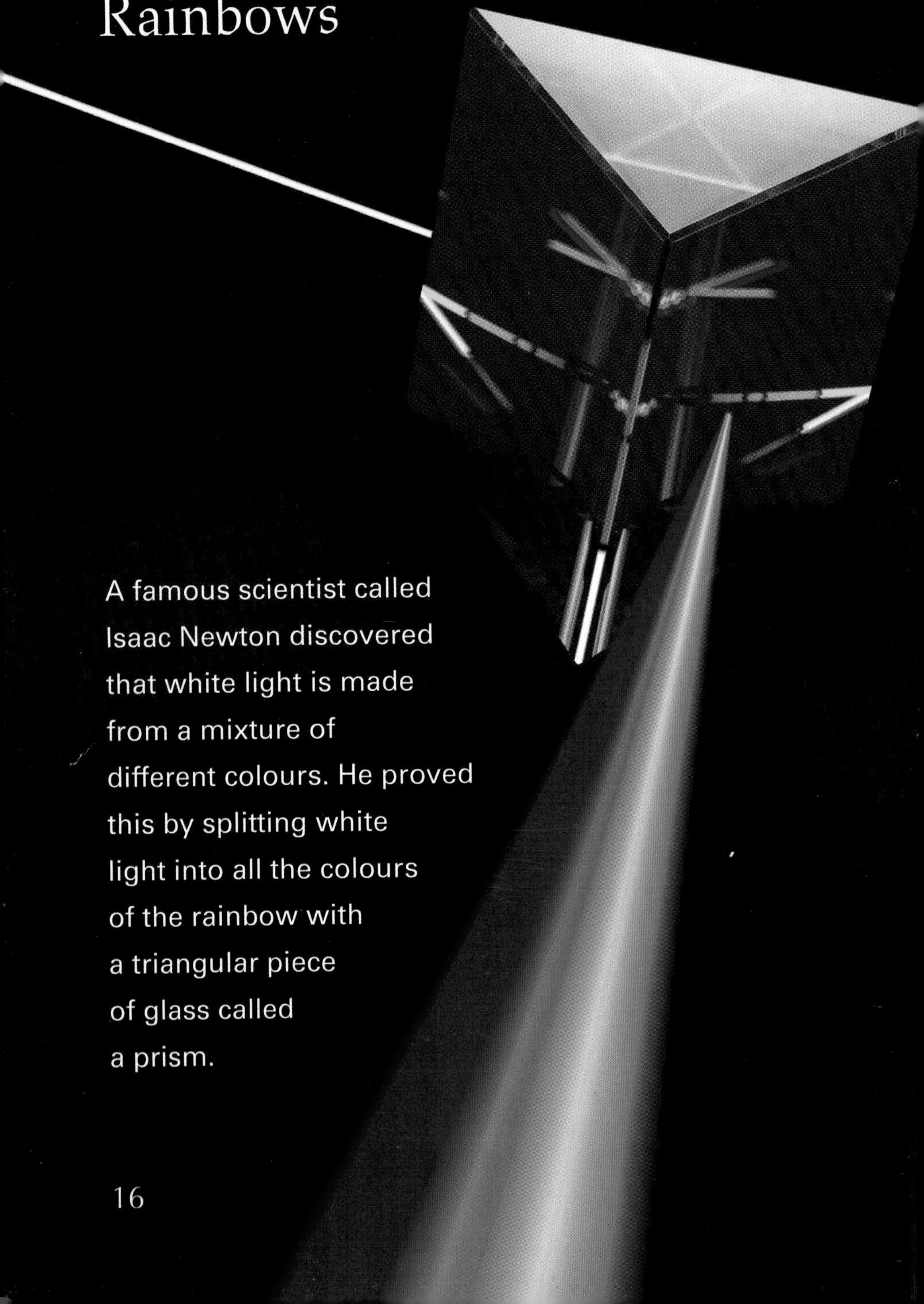

A famous scientist called
Isaac Newton discovered
that white light is made
from a mixture of
different colours. He proved
this by splitting white
light into all the colours
of the rainbow with
a triangular piece
of glass called
a prism.

The prism slows down the white light and each of the colours within the white light changes direction slightly (refracts) as they pass into the prism. When the light comes out of the other side of the prism it has been separated into colours.

The same thing happens when light shines through rain droplets in the air. The light is refracted inside the rain droplets just like a prism. That's why when it's raining and sunny at the same time, we sometimes see a rainbow.

You might see rainbows in waterfalls or fountains on a sunny day too. The water droplets are refracting the white light and splitting it into colours.

The Sun's light is refracted through rain droplets to create a rainbow.

Travelling light

Light travels faster than anything we know about in the universe. It travels at around 300 thousand km per second or 700 million miles an hour.

It's quite hard to imagine just how fast that is. The Sun is around 150 million km away from Earth. That is the same distance as if you ran 3733 times round Earth! But light from the Sun takes only eight minutes to reach us.

There are other stars in the sky that are much further away than the Sun. It takes their light many years to travel to Earth. We call the distance light travels in one year a light year. It's 9,500,000,000,000 kilometres.

Some stars are 50 light years away so if we see them exploding now, we are actually seeing what happened 50 years ago.

Or if we're looking at a star that's 500 light years away, we're seeing what happened 500 years ago. All thanks to light! It is as if we're looking back in time – and that star might not even be there any more!

looking back in time

Sun and Earth

exploding star

Einstein

Einstein was a famous scientist. One of his theories was that the laws of **physics** were the same everywhere in the Universe. Using mathematics, he suggested everything in the universe, you, me, animals, plants, planets, stars – everything depends on the speed of light.

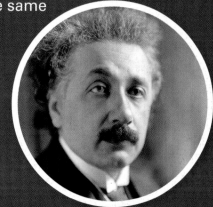

Lightning

Lightning is a giant electric spark.

Static electricity builds up inside clouds when ice **particles** rub against each other. When there is enough electric charge a spark either jumps through the cloud causing sheet lightning, or between the cloud and the ground, causing fork lightning.

Lightning always finds the fastest way to connect with the ground, so it will strike tall trees or high buildings. Engineers fit lightning conductors to tall buildings to allow the electrical charge to connect with Earth safely, protecting the building in the event of a lightning strike.

a lightning conductor running up a tall spire

Thunder

Thunder is the sound of the giant electrical spark heating up the air around it. The air becomes so hot that it expands very quickly, making a bang.

Usually in thunderstorms, we see lightning flash and then hear the bang of the thunder afterwards. That's because it takes longer for the sound to travel to us. Sound waves travel a million times slower than light waves. If however, the storm is directly above us, we hear thunder and see the flash at nearly the same time because the sound and light don't travel far before they reach us.

Lightning in space

Earth isn't the only planet with lightning. **Astronomers** have seen massive storms in the swirling gasses on Jupiter and lightning flashes in the dark clouds of Venus.

lightning on Venus

The Sun

The Sun is a star that's close enough to Earth for us to see it during the day. It is roughly spherical and gives out light and heat which helps plants to grow and creates the perfect temperature for life on Earth.

The Sun

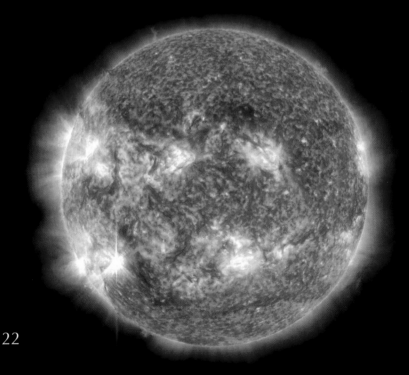

Fact File

- *Size:* diameter: 1,392,684 km (you could fit 109 planet Earths in a row across the Sun)
- *Age:* 4.6 billion years
- *Surface temperature:* 5500 °C
- *Mass:* 1,989,100,000,000,000,000,000 billion kg (333,060 × the mass of Earth)
- *Distance from Earth:* 149.6 million km
- *Made of:* gas, mostly hydrogen and helium

Sunburn

When sunlight shines on our skin it helps our bodies to make the vitamin D we need to keep our bones and teeth healthy. But if we get too much bright sunlight on our skin it burns us. It is the ultraviolet rays from the Sun that cause sunburn. When we cover up with clothes or put on sun cream, we block the UV rays and stop them being absorbed by our skin.

Sunglasses

The light from the Sun is so bright that it would damage our eyes if we looked straight at it. Sunglasses are translucent so they let some of the Sun's rays through but reflect many of the rays away. They let us see when it's bright and protect our eyes at the same time.

Earth, Sun and Moon

Although it doesn't feel like it, the Earth is spinning around and travelling through space!

Night and day

Every day the Earth spins around once on its **axis**. Each complete rotation takes 24 hours.

axis

As we rotate away from the Sun's light rays and move into its shadow it starts to get dark. Once Earth is turned completely away from the Sun and is totally in shadow it is our night-time. While we're sleeping, people living on the other side of the planet are facing the Sun so it's their daytime.

light from the Sun

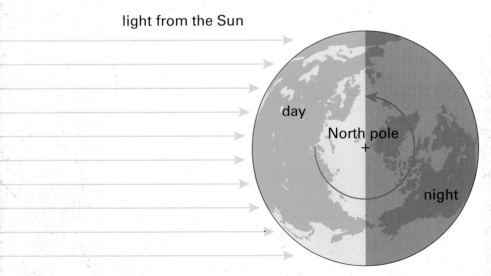

day

North pole

night

or orbit, takes 365 days – a year. So if you are ten years old, you have travelled around the Sun ten times already!

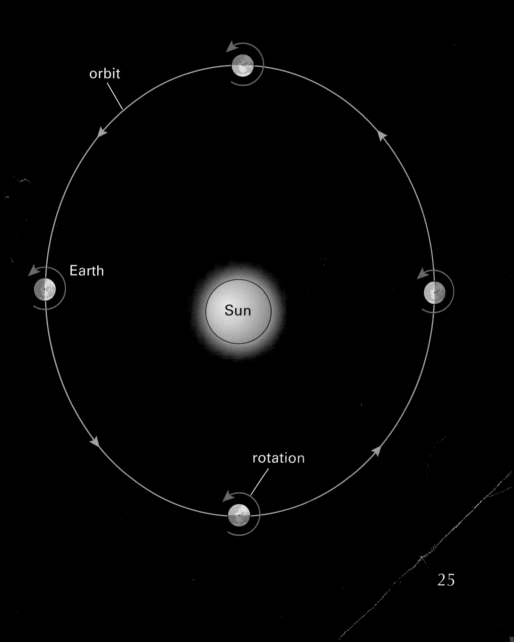

orbit

Earth

Sun

rotation

People used to think the Earth was the centre of the universe – they thought everything in space rotated around it. We call this a geocentric model of the universe. They saw the Sun rise in the east and set in the west and assumed it was orbiting around Earth. But they were wrong.

Galileo

Several scientists had proposed a new idea where the Earth rotated around the Sun. This is called a heliocentric model of the universe. Galileo was the scientist who actually proved

Galileo Galilei

it was true with observations as well as mathematics. He made a telescope good enough to see four of the moons of Jupiter. He could see their positions changing and he realised they were orbiting around Jupiter and not around Earth.

Galileo's telescope

This proved that people had got the wrong idea and later he went on to show the Sun was at the centre of our solar system, that moons rotate around planets, and the Earth and planets rotate around the Sun. Despite the evidence, it took a long time before people believed him.

Galileo was arrested for his claims about space because his views were so different to what everyone else thought at the time.

Fact File

The Moon

The Moon orbits around Earth and each orbit takes about a month. The Moon is not a source of light like the Sun; we can only see the Moon when the Sun's light reflects off it. Depending on which stage of the orbit the Moon is at, different parts of the Moon are lit up by the Sun's light. When the Moon appears as a crescent shape in the sky, it is because the rest of it is in shadow. When we see a full Moon we are seeing the Sun's light reflecting off the whole surface of the Moon that's facing towards us.

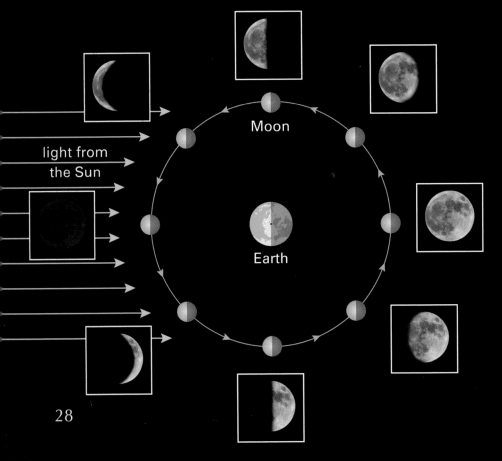

light from the Sun

Moon

Earth

Lunar eclipse

A lunar eclipse happens when a full Moon moves behind
the Earth with the Sun on the opposite side and the Earth's
shadow covers the Moon.

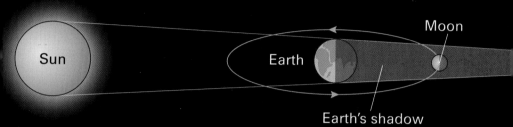

Sun

Earth

Moon

Earth's shadow

The dark shadowed area of the Moon gets bigger
and bigger until the whole Moon is in shadow and
it appears red. That's because the red part of
the Sun's light gets refracted through
the Earth's atmosphere
towards the Moon.

the stages of
a lunar eclipse

As the Moon begins
to move behind
the Earth in a lunar
eclipse it looks as if someone
has taken a bite out of it!

Fact
File

Solar eclipse

A solar eclipse is when the Moon passes in front of the Sun as we see them from Earth.

The Sun is 400 times bigger than the Moon but because it is 400 times further away from Earth, they take up exactly the same amount of space in our sky. This amazing coincidence of sizes and distances can result in a solar eclipse. They happen very rarely because everything needs to line up just perfectly. When it does, for a short time it becomes dark on Earth during the day as we enter into the Moon's shadow.

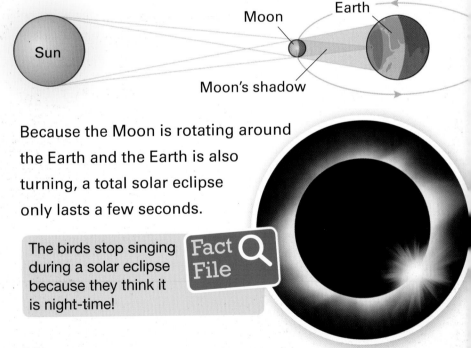

Because the Moon is rotating around the Earth and the Earth is also turning, a total solar eclipse only lasts a few seconds.

The birds stop singing during a solar eclipse because they think it is night-time!

Fact File

Northern Lights

The Sun creates spectacular coloured lights that can be seen in the night sky called the Northern Lights (or Aurora Borealis). Charged particles from the Sun's surface travel to Earth and interact with gases in the Earth's atmosphere to create light. The colours we see are different depending on the gases the particles meet – oxygen creates yellow and green colours, nitrogen makes red and hydrogen and helium make purple and blue.

the Northern Lights seen in Iceland

On the other side of planet Earth in Australia they see the Southern Lights.

Fact File

31

Visible and invisible light

There are many different types of light from the Sun that we cannot see. Together, the visible and invisible light make up the **electromagnetic spectrum**.

The light we can't see is useful for lots of things.

Microwaves

Microwaves are a type of invisible light energy. We use them to heat up food. Microwaves work by vibrating the liquid contained in the food. As the liquid vibrates, the food quickly heats up.

gamma rays

X-rays

ultraviolet light

violet

visible light

red

infrared light

microwaves

radio waves

more energy

bigger wavelength

Radio waves

If we move past the red light in the electromagnetic spectrum we find radio waves. Radio waves have bigger wiggles – or wavelengths – than red light. We can't see these waves but we can pick them up through our radios – they are mostly used for communication. So if you tune a radio and listen to a local FM station you are picking up a signal being transmitted by radio waves. Police use Walkie Talkie radios to transmit radio wave messages from one place to another.

Radio waves are also used to transmit mobile phones signals, GPS locations and Wi-Fi signals. They have many uses in medicine too including scanning patients and taking pictures of their bodies.

We can detect radio waves from stars and make pictures of them using radio telescopes.  Fact File

Ultraviolet light

If we move past violet light to smaller wavelengths we get to UV or ultraviolet light. UV light comes from the Sun and can be harmful if we get too much of it on our skin. Although we cannot see ultraviolet light, some animals can. Flowers have UV markings on their petals to attract bees, flies and butterflies. The markings are a bit like lights on a runway and they show the insects where to land.

a dandelion in normal light (top) and UV light (bottom)

Fact File

When we shine a UV light onto dull looking scorpions they glow a bright blue-green.

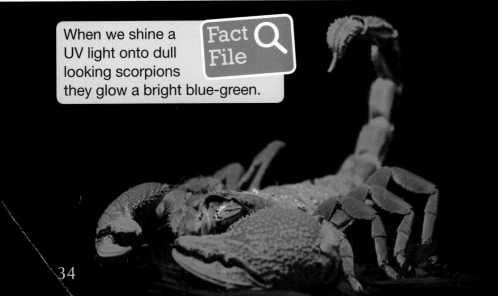

The wasp spider decorates its web with zigzags of UV silk to imitate patterns in flowers. The UV decorations trick insects into flying into the web where they get stuck.

Birds of prey called kestrels hunt tiny rodents called voles. Kestrels hover high up in the air looking down to try to spot the voles. They can see the voles' fresh **urine** glowing with UV light and that helps them to locate a vole.

We can see UV light by using UV lamps that make UV colours glow.

Infrared

Infrared rays are given off by anything warm so your body is emitting infrared waves right now! Snakes can see in infrared and this is very useful when they're hunting – their prey glows in the undergrowth, making it easier to see and catch.

Scientists and photographers use infrared-sensitive cameras and goggles to see things when it's dark. This technology allows them to track animals and people by the heat given off from their bodies.

a mouse seen in infrared light

Volcanologists monitor volcanoes using infrared cameras to see how hot the lava is to help predict eruptions.

Fact File

This technology can also be used to see where buildings are losing heat so people know what draughtproofing and insulation are needed to reduce heat loss and save money on heating bills.

X-rays and shadows

X-rays are another type of invisible light energy. Visible light is stopped by human skin, but X-rays can pass through skin and fat in our bodies. However they are stopped by bones.

When a **radiographer** shines X-rays through a person's hand they take a picture showing the shadows made by the bones. Normally we can't see bones because they're hidden but X-rays allow us to see inside our bodies using shadows. This picture – an X-ray – shows doctors if any of the bones are cracked or broken.

Light in the past

As well as natural light from the Sun, we can make our own light sources. When materials get hot they give off light. The first fires we made were created by rubbing sticks together or chipping flint to make a hot spark. That spark lit a fire which was used to cook food and to provide a source of light at night.

Candles

The first candles were made by the Romans. They used fat from cows and sheep to make wax and cloth or string for the wick. Now most candles are made from oils from plants mixed with paraffin (which comes from oil).

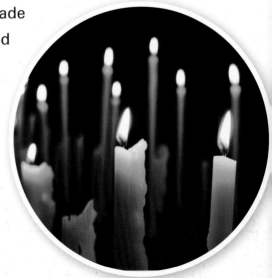

Lamps

The first oil lamps were made from natural hollow shapes like seashells and coconuts. The earliest stone oil lamp discovered is over 10,000 years old. These early lamps contained whale oil or olive oil with a wick dipped into it. The oil soaked into the wick and when it was lit it burnt slowly, giving off light.

Signalling

Lamps were important for signalling and navigating at sea before we had **GPS navigation systems**. Oil lamps in lighthouses told ships where the land was and stopped them running into rocks in the dark.

Electric lights

In electric lights, a flow of electricity causes gases in a tube to heat up and glow, giving off light. Electricity is a type of energy.

energy saving lightbulb

To make an electric light work, electricity travels to the light bulb along cables made from metals. Metals let electric charge flow through them easily which makes them good conductors. A flow of electric charge is called a current.

Here's a circuit diagram showing how an electric current powers a light bulb.

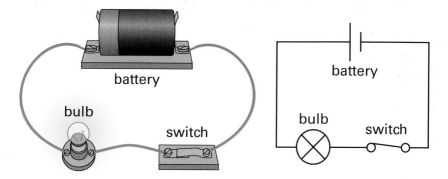

The light bulb will only light if you close the switch to complete the circuit. The battery makes electricity but the current has to flow from one end of the battery to the other to make the light work. The different sides of the battery have different charges, positive and negative, and the current flows between them in a wire.

We use electricity to power the electric lights in our lives.

Solar power

Solar power is electricity that is made from the Sun's light. The two main ways to make solar power are using solar cells or using mirrors which concentrate the Sun's power.

Solar cells

Solar cells convert the Sun's energy into electrical energy. Solar cells work in all weathers; all they need is light. The dark coloured materials in a solar cell absorb the Sun's light rays and an electric current flows between different materials in the cell. Many solar cells make up a solar panel and we place solar panels on roofs to help power homes.

Solar cells are used to help power satellites in space.

Concentrated solar power

Concentrated solar power plants use different patterns of mirrors to reflect the Sun's light into tubes of liquids which heat up and make steam. The steam turns a turbine around which generates electricity.

Renewable energy

Solar power is a type of renewable energy. That means it's not going to run out because we know the Sun will keep shining for at least another 4 billion years.

Animal lights

Some animals can make their own light in a chemical reaction called **bioluminescence**. This chemical reaction releases light energy in their bodies to confuse **predators**, attract prey, send signals and attract mates.

Organisms that use bioluminescence include jellyfish, sharks, fungi, beetles, corals, worms and shrimps. Some tiny bacteria are bioluminescent too.

Fireflies

Fireflies create light by adding oxygen from the air to chemicals in their bodies, flashing a light on and off as they fly around. They flash their lights to attract a mate.

Fireflies are actually beetles, not flies.

Fact File

Angler fish

Angler fish live deep in the ocean, where the Sun's light rays can't reach. They create their own light source, on a stalk coming out of their foreheads. Fish are attracted to the light and swim right towards the angler fish's mouth!

Some tiny sea creatures called plankton squirt glowing liquid into the water to confuse predators. It usually glows blue but can sometimes glow green, red, or orange. Predators then try to attack the bioluminescent chemicals in the water instead of the plankton.

Other types of plankton glow to attract a mate, a bit like fireflies.

Photosynthesis

Plants use light to make their own food.

Cells in their leaves capture sunlight. The leaves also absorb carbon dioxide from the air and they mix it with water and minerals drawn up from the ground using energy from the light. The process of turning water and carbon dioxide into food using light is called photosynthesis.

There is a chemical in plant leaves called chlorophyll. It makes the leaves look green and helps them to absorb sunlight.

Fact File

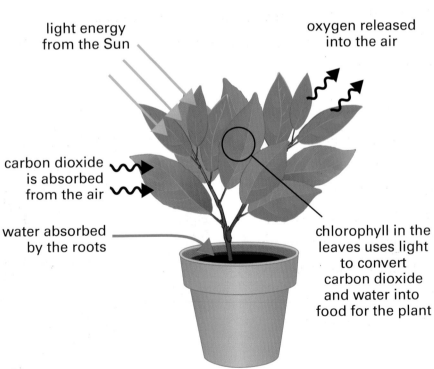

light energy from the Sun

oxygen released into the air

carbon dioxide is absorbed from the air

water absorbed by the roots

chlorophyll in the leaves uses light to convert carbon dioxide and water into food for the plant

The food a plant makes is a sugar called glucose.
This sugar helps the plant to grow more leaves and catch
more light.

Plants are brilliant!

When plants are taking in
carbon dioxide gas they
release oxygen into
the atmosphere, which
humans and animals need
to breathe. Plants are also
a rich source of food for
humans and animals.

Food chains

All living things need food. A food chain shows how living things depend on each other in order to survive. At the start of every food chain is the Sun's light.

Plants in the food chain are called producers because they produce their own food through photosynthesis, using the Sun's light. Animals are called consumers because they consume or eat plants and other animals. Each part in the food chain – starting with light from the Sun – gives energy to the next link in the chain. The arrows simply mean "gives energy to".

the Sun

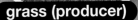

grass (producer)

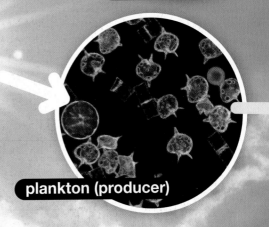

plankton (producer)

Animals that eat other animals are called predators.
The animals that they eat are called prey. Predators are
at the top of the food chain and the Sun is at the start
of the food chain. So even though a lion doesn't eat
the Sun, it survives because of the Sun. The zebra the lion
feeds on will eat plants and those plants make food from
the Sun's light.

Food chains show us that life on Earth depends on light.

zebra (consumer)

lion (predator)

small fish (consumer)

shark (predator)

Light in the future

There are many exciting uses for light in the future.

Artificial eye retina

Scientists are developing an artificial eye
retina to help people who can't see. It is
a light-sensitive, flexible film that absorbs
light and sends an electrical signal to
the brain so it will work just like a real retina.

Lasers

Lasers are concentrated beams of light. They can be used
for many things including cutting diamonds and making
precision operations in surgery.

Doctors can now sew up wounds
using light. A laser heats up the skin
around the wound causing the cells
in the skin to stick together. It doesn't
leave a scar and there's no need for
stitches or staples.

Night vision

We can already buy cars that have infrared technology in
the windscreen allowing us to see further into the night
than the light from our car headlights would allow us
to see. This technology could end up in glasses too!

Invisibility

Invisibility has always fascinated us! Scientists are creating invisibility in different ways. One is using fibre optic technology to bend light around things, rather than reflecting off them and into our eyes. The other is creating invisibility cloaks that change the way light reflects off objects so that we can't see the size or shape of whatever is under the cloak, it just looks like a flat surface!

Mirrors in space

Mirrors in space could help reduce the amount of sunlight entering into our Earth's atmosphere by reflecting it back out into space. This could reverse global warming of planet Earth that's currently being caused by a build-up of gases in the Earth's atmosphere.

Solar power

One day the Sun might be our main source of electricity with huge solar panels on Earth and in space. Ultimately all life depends on sunlight. Whatever our future, light will always be an essential part of life.

Glossary

archaeologists   scientists who examine old objects and places to find out about life in the past

astronomers   scientists who study space, the stars and planets

axis   the imaginary line that the Earth rotates around

bioluminescence   the production of light by living things

cells   the basic structure that makes up living things. Cells are tiny

cone   cell in the eye that is sensitive to colour in daylight

electromagnetic spectrum   the range of electromagnetic radiation from the Sun which includes visible light

energy   power to do work and make things happen. Light, heat and electricity are types of energy.

GPS navigation system   a device which uses satellites in orbit to calculate its location on the Earth.

magnify   to make something appear larger than it is using a lens or a microscope

opaque   a material that light cannot pass through

particles   extremely small pieces of matter including atoms and parts of atoms.

periscopes   a device which uses mirrors to allow the user to view objects that are not in the direct line of sight

physics   the science of properties of matter and energy

predators   animals that kill other animals for food

radiographer   a person who operates X-ray machines

retina   the light sensitive lining at the back of the eye

rod   cell in the eye that is sensitive to dim light but not colour

static electricity   electric charge produced by friction between objects

translucent   a material that allows some light to pass through

transparent   a material that allows all light to pass through

ultraviolet   a non-visible part of the electromagnetic spectrum

urine   waste that the body expels as fluid, also known as wee

Index

Sources of light

natural

Northern Lights

the Sun

lightning

bioluminescence

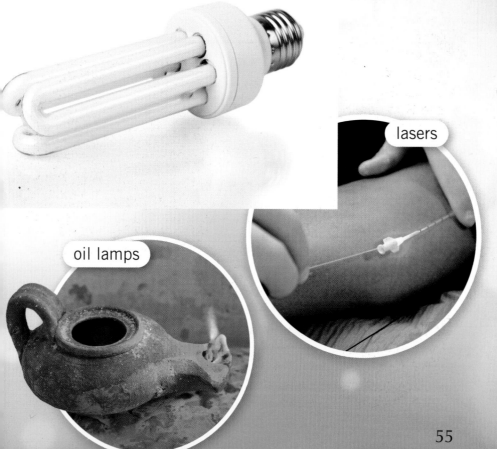

man-made

candles

lasers

oil lamps

Ideas for reading

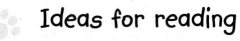

Written by Clare Dowdall, PhD
Lecturer and Primary Literacy Consultant

Reading objectives:
- make comparisons within and across books
- discuss their understanding
- summarise the main ideas drawn from more than one paragraph, identifying key details that support the main ideas
- retrieve, record and present information from non-fiction

Spoken language objectives:
- give well-structured descriptions, explanations and narratives for different purposes

Curriculum links: Science – light

Resources: torches, modelling clay and pencils; cardboard tubes and mirrors, pencils and paper.

Build a context for reading
- Look around the room for light sources. Ask children to tell you any facts that they know about light, and its properties.
- Look at the front cover and read the blurb together. Look closely at the images of the trees and prism. Ask children what could be happening to the light in both images.
- Challenge children to answer the first blurb question: *What exactly is light?* Collect their ideas on a whiteboard.

Understand and apply reading strategies
- Ask children to read pp2–3. Challenge them to tell you, in their own words, what light is – based on their reading. Compare their ideas with the list on the whiteboard.
- Introduce a close reading strategy. Ask children to reread pp2–3 to find and list as many different facts as they can about light. Compare their ideas, and see who has found the most facts.